TALENT MAGNET

HOW TO ATTRACT AND KEEP THE BEST PEOPLE

QUICK START GUIDE
MARK MILLER & RANDY GRAVITT

Copyright 2018 © CFA Properties, Inc.
and InteGREAT Leadership™

All rights reserved. No part of this publication may be reproduced, distributed, or transmitted in any form or by any means, including photocopying, recording, or other electronic or mechanical methods, without the prior written permission of the author, except in the case of brief quotations embodied in critical reviews and certain other noncommercial uses permitted by copyright law. For permission requests, write to **INFO@INTEGREATLEADERSHIP.COM.**

Printed in the United States of America
Design and Layout by Eliza Robson and Lindsay Miller

Printing Information
Bennett Graphics
125 Royal Woods Court, Suite 100
Tucker, GA 30084

Tel: (770) 723-1192
www.BennettGraphics.com

ISBN 978-0-9998210-1-5

CONTENTS

WELCOME	4
SECTION ONE: BETTER BOSS	6
DEMONSTRATE CARE	8
STAY ENGAGED	12
LEAD WELL	16
SECTION TWO: BRIGHTER FUTURE	20
CHAMPION GROWTH	22
PROVIDE CHALLENGE	26
PROMOTE OPPORTUNITY	30
SECTION THREE: BIGGER VISION	34
ENSURE ALIGNMENT	36
FOSTER CONNECTION	40
CELEBRATE IMPACT	44
SECTION FOUR: TELL THE STORY	48
BE PROACTIVE	50
EMBRACE TECHNOLOGY	54
DEPUTIZE EVERYONE	58
ADDITIONAL RESOURCES	62

WELCOME

Talk to any good leader, and you will find someone who understands the importance of being fully staffed; however, the best leaders have set a higher standard… in a High Performance Organization, the goal is to attract and retain Top Talent. But wait, who is Top Talent and why would your organization want more of them?

Look in the mirror – Top Talent looks a lot like you. You are the best of the best; you are engaged, disciplined, focused on people and performance; you show initiative and demonstrate concern for your fellow workers. You are the type of person others want to work with. You bring energy to the work.

Your organization wants more people like you, because Top Talent creates competitive advantage, is more agile, produces better results, responds well to complexity, represents the brand, accelerates growth, and ultimately attracts more Top Talent.

The *Talent Magnet Quick Start Guide* has been created as a supplemental resource for the *Talent Magnet* book and Field Guide. It is your daily companion to help you better understand the attributes Top Talent finds most important and outline practical actions you can take to build your own Talent Magnet.

Any organization can say the things Top Talent wants to hear, but without day-to-day leadership, your promise may never become reality. You are the key to creating a workplace so attractive, Top Talent will be standing in line to work with your organization. With your focused, daily commitment, your organization can become a Talent Magnet!

LET'S GET STARTED…

BETTER BOSS

SECTION ONE

Who wants a bad boss? Actually, no one. However, the caliber of the boss is a condition of employment for Top Talent. A **BETTER BOSS** is one who is available, engaged, and committed to adding value to everyone he or she leads.

Acquiring and keeping Top Talent can become your ultimate competitive advantage. If you truly intend to become a Talent Magnet, start with a decision to be a **BETTER BOSS.**

For a full overview of Better Boss, please reference the Talent Magnet Field Guide.

BEST PRACTICE
DEMONSTRATE CARE

Once you realize Top Talent is looking for a Better Boss, the next step is to become one. The question is, "How?" Being a better leader begins with a foundation of caring. Unless you genuinely care for people, you will struggle to attract high performers. But it is not enough to simply care in your mind and heart, you must **DEMONSTRATE CARE** with your actions.

As the leader, the onus is on you to frequently communicate how much people matter. You really can be a Better Boss and create a thriving environment where the best of the best wants to work. Make a decision to **DEMONSTRATE CARE,** and you will be on your way.

KEY CONCEPT 1

DEMONSTRATE CARE TOWARD THOSE YOU LEAD.

Being a better leader begins with a foundation of caring. Unless you genuinely care for people you will struggle to attract high performers. You must Demonstrate Care if you hope to create an attractive culture.

KEY CONCEPT 2

ONE SIZE DOES NOT FIT ALL.

Demonstrating Care can take on many forms. From creating role clarity to providing feedback, leaders can Demonstrate Care by conveying they are interested in the success of their team members.

KEY CONCEPT 3

CARE MUST BE EXPRESSED FREQUENTLY.

Taking the time to show you are interested in what your team members are interested in communicates tremendous value. Getting to know their families, backgrounds, and dreams shows you genuinely value them as people.

THINGS YOU CAN DO TO DEMONSTRATE CARE

☐ **FIVE & FIVE**

Schedule a 10-minute walk or other time alone with each employee. Spend the first five minutes learning about their life outside of work. The next five should be allocated to any feedback they have for you.

DATE COMPLETED: _____

☐ **PRAISE CHECK**

Take advantage of the regular schedule of payroll to add a quick personal note to your employees' physical/digital paychecks.

DATE COMPLETED: _____

☐ SHOUT-OUT

Leave a personalized message for a team member in some place visible to other team members – birthdays, job well done, etc.

DATE COMPLETED: _____

☐ TRAVELING TROPHY

Create a traveling trophy (e.g., golden object, special badge, figurine, etc.) that moves employee to employee based on being "caught" doing something outstanding.

DATE COMPLETED: _____

☐ WALL OF FAME

Create a "Wall of Fame." Post customer compliments, charts/graphs depicting positive progress, copies of certificates (e.g., training completed, awards, acknowledgment of achievement), peer-to-peer notes of thanks, etc.

DATE COMPLETED: _____

BEST PRACTICE
STAY ENGAGED

Why do some organizations prosper while others plateau? The answer is usually found in how well they are led and in how much talent they have. As the leader, you have the ability to impact both. But in the eyes of your people, your ability to lead well is contingent on your level of engagement. A Better Boss must **STAY ENGAGED.**

Your responsibility is to lean in and **STAY ENGAGED.** When you do, you meet one of Top Talent's most often stated expectations of their leaders: Showing up in reality – never just going through the motions.

KEY CONCEPT 1

THERE IS NO SUBSTITUTE FOR SHOWING UP.

To be a Better Boss requires you to be present, and your presence is not something you can delegate. You must be visible and remain involved in the real work of your people.

KEY CONCEPT 2

LEADERS WILLING TO "DO REAL WORK" GENERATE RESPECT.

There are many ways leaders can be involved in the day-to-day operation of their team; examples include: staying focused in meetings, listening to the opinions of others, asking good questions and accepting responsibility when things go wrong.

KEY CONCEPT 3

THE BEST LEADERS ARE GROUNDED IN REALITY.

You must stay connected to what is really happening in your organization. If you are out of touch, your presence is irrelevant. What are the current challenges your organization is facing? What are your people struggling with?

THINGS YOU CAN DO TO **STAY ENGAGED**

☐ **START/STOP SURVEY**

Collect anonymous feedback from your team members about your performance: What should I start doing? What should I stop doing? Identify opportunities for growth, and share ideas inspired by the feedback with your team.

DATE COMPLETED: _____

☐ **TEAM TIME**

Make it a routine practice to show up for meetings conducted by your team. Even a brief appearance will give you an opportunity to connect with your people.

DATE COMPLETED: _____

☐ YESTERDAY - TODAY - TOMORROW

Conduct a five-minute team huddle. Quickly recap yesterday's accomplishments, today's challenges, and tomorrow's goals.

DATE COMPLETED: _____

☐ COMMENT BOX

Set up a classic anonymous comment box – with a twist. Provide 3x5 index cards to your team members, and encourage them to anonymously share an idea for leadership to work on over the next 30 days.

DATE COMPLETED: _____

☐ OFFICE HOURS

Dedicate 1-2 hours a week to be available to your team members for one-on-one meetings. Be consistently available during this period to answer their questions or provide assistance. Let them set the agenda.

DATE COMPLETED: _____

BEST PRACTICE
LEAD WELL

Bad leadership has been the downfall of many organizations. One of its consequences: impeding your ability to attract Top Talent. If you want to fill your team with high performers, you must **LEAD WELL.**

The most effective leaders are servant leaders. The attitude of your heart will ultimately have the greatest impact on your ability to **LEAD WELL** - admitting mistakes, sharing credit, maintaining a spirit of humility, being courageous and thinking others first all reflect your readiness to lead.

Do you really want to be a Better Boss capable of attracting a team of Top Talent? Commit to a life-long journey of learning to **LEAD WELL.**

KEY CONCEPT 1

TOP TALENT EXPECTS TO BE WELL LED.

To be effective, leaders must master the fundamentals. Like blocking and tackling are essential to win in football, casting vision, engaging people, reinventing systems, valuing people and performance, and walking the talk are all required to win Top Talent.

KEY CONCEPT 2

THE BEST LEADERS ARE SERVANT LEADERS.

The servant leader is compelled by an unshakeable desire to serve others. Daily, those who wish to be a servant leader must confront this challenge: Will I be a serving leader or a self-serving one?

KEY CONCEPT 3

SKILLS ALONE ARE NEVER ENOUGH.

If your heart is not right, no one cares about your skills. Admitting mistakes, taking ownership, being vulnerable, and sharing credit will go a long way toward improving your leadership.

THINGS YOU CAN DO TO LEAD WELL

☐ BOX TOP

If you don't already have one, invest the time to create a vision or mission statement for your organization. Show your team and potential new hires the "box top" for the puzzle you are trying to put together.

DATE COMPLETED: _____

☐ NEW & IMPROVED

Ask your leaders to help you identify one area for improvement. Consider this approach: If we changed _____ over the next 30 days, our performance would improve drastically. Identify it and do it!

DATE COMPLETED: _____

☐ TEAM LEADERSHIP

Assess the health of your team by asking each member to rate the effectiveness of the group. Make plans to strengthen any weak areas surfaced by the team.

DATE COMPLETED: _____

☐ THE POWER OF AND

Identify two opposing challenges in your business (speed and hospitality, or quality and low-cost, etc.). Begin to actively pursue BOTH. There's tremendous power in the tension.

DATE COMPLETED: _____

☐ VALUES MATTER

Work with your leaders to identify your top four to six core values – the beliefs you want to drive the daily behaviors of your team. Ask your leaders to create a communication plan to cascade these throughout your entire team.

DATE COMPLETED: _____

BRIGHTER FUTURE

SECTION TWO

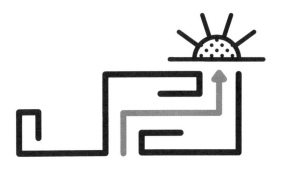

One of the most important considerations for Top Talent when deciding where to work is the impact of today's job on tomorrow's opportunities. Top Talent is always pursuing a **BRIGHTER FUTURE.**

The point is not to think of one idealized **BRIGHTER FUTURE** and attempt to deliver it; the definition will vary from person to person. What is required from you is a commitment to help your most talented people become the architects of their own future. Then you will be well on your way to becoming a Talent Magnet!

For a full overview of Brighter Future, please reference the Talent Magnet Field Guide.

BEST PRACTICE
CHAMPION GROWTH

If your goal is to help Top Talent live into a Brighter Future, you will undoubtedly do countless things over the years to assist them including: resource, challenge, coach, and encourage. However, nothing will be more important than your continuing efforts to **CHAMPION GROWTH.**

Wise leaders understand to become a Talent Magnet they must **CHAMPION GROWTH.**

KEY CONCEPT 1

LEADERS SHOULD EXPECT EVERYONE TO GROW.

Healthy things grow – plants, animals, organizations, and people. As a leader, you are uniquely positioned to help people grow. To Champion Growth means you will fight for, defend, promote, assist, and expect people to grow.

KEY CONCEPT 2

EVERY PERSON NEEDS A WRITTEN DEVELOPMENT PLAN

When you write something down or type it in your computer, it takes on new form and meaning; ideas transform, they become more tangible and more real. When people have written development plans, something amazing happens…they grow!

KEY CONCEPT 3

ACCOUNTABILITY IS ESSENTIAL TO GROWTH.

When we give someone the gift of accountability, we help them reach their goals and more. One of the most satisfying parts of your job as a leader will be helping people reach their full potential – often, far more than they ever believed possible.

THINGS YOU CAN DO TO CHAMPION GROWTH

☐ COACHING CHATS

Assign each team member a manager or leader to be their "coach." Encourage weekly or bi-weekly check-ins for the coach to learn more about the team member's goals, interests, and challenges.

DATE COMPLETED: _____

☐ LUNCH AND LEARN

Dedicate one lunch hour each month to delve into a development area or specific skill with your team members. Select a leader or find an external expert to facilitate a conversation on the assigned topic.

DATE COMPLETED: _____

☐ GOLD FUND

Allocate "GOLD" funds annually for every team member to provide Growth, Opportunity, Learning, and Development. Employees can invest the allowance on approved activities that accelerate their personal growth.

DATE COMPLETED: _____

☐ MENTOR MATCHMAKER

Create a speed dating set-up during a lunch hour to facilitate one-on-one conversations between senior and junior employees. Encourage leaders to follow-up with junior employees who show an interest in continuing the conversation.

DATE COMPLETED: _____

☐ STEPPING STONES

Provide an Individual Development Plan for employees to monitor and improve their own performance throughout the year. The plan should provide a path to achieve measurable development goals and contain a realistic timeframe for achieving each goal.

DATE COMPLETED: _____

BEST PRACTICE
PROVIDE CHALLENGE

Our research revealed a high likelihood someone in your organizational life has been willing to **PROVIDE CHALLENGE.** This is an indispensable part of the growth process. None of us can reach our full potential without someone willing to call out the best in us. Challenge is required for humans to thrive.

If you honestly hope to attract Top Talent, don't neglect to **PROVIDE CHALLENGE.**

KEY CONCEPT 1

TOP TALENT WANTS TO BE CHALLENGED.

Providing challenge can begin by helping people raise their own sights. Virtually all of us have a story of someone who saw more in us than we saw in ourselves and inspired us to grow.

KEY CONCEPT 2

STRETCH ASSIGNMENTS ACCELERATE GROWTH.

Many of us can remember the day we were challenged to think differently, work harder, or change our behavior. Sometimes, all that was required was a leader to shine a light on something for us. These are the conversations Top Talent wants and needs.

KEY CONCEPT 3

CANDOR IS ESSENTIAL TO GROWTH.

From time to time, you will find yourself in a situation in which a hard conversation is needed. If you sugarcoat the truth or dodge the issues preventing Top Talent from soaring, you will both regret it.

THINGS YOU CAN DO TO PROVIDE CHALLENGE

☐ **REAL FEEDBACK**

Schedule a session with every member of your team and give them real feedback on their performance. Challenge each with a specific area for improvement.

DATE COMPLETED: _____

☐ **POP QUIZ**

Encourage your team to memorize your vision/mission and values. Periodically and unannounced, ask members of your team to tell you about the vision/mission or quiz them on your core values.

DATE COMPLETED: _____

☐ THINKING PARTNER

Bring an employee into a real meeting to play an active "step up" role. Ask him or her to listen and contribute. "Putting them on the spot" can help them grow.

DATE COMPLETED: _____

☐ HERO CHALLENGE

Think of someone who inspired you to grow – maybe a parent, a coach, a teacher, a former boss, or even a colleague. Identify traits and characteristics of that person you want to emulate in your life.

DATE COMPLETED: _____

☐ REWRITE THE SCRIPT

Challenge yourself to recall a difficult conversation from your past. As best you can, write out the dialogue. Next, re-write the interaction to create a more productive outcome. Apply your thinking to future scenarios.

DATE COMPLETED: _____

BEST PRACTICE
PROMOTE OPPORTUNITY

When Top Talent considers a job, they are often thinking far down the road – sometimes even thinking about future employers! This is why we say they are looking for a place in the present that can help them ensure a Brighter Future.

Hold Top Talent loosely; serve as scouts for their future. When you **PROMOTE OPPORTUNITY,** they will flourish and retention should improve. They may ultimately leave, but if they do, they will leave you and your team stronger as a result of their contributions.

KEY CONCEPT 1

IN GREAT ORGANIZATIONS TALENT IS SHARED FREELY.

You can serve as an "opportunity broker" for your people. This is in stark contrast to the leaders who attempt to hoard and sequester talent from the organization.

KEY CONCEPT 2

TOP TALENT IS ALWAYS SEEKING OPPORTUNITY.

Top Talent has more of a future orientation than most people. They see the future full of promise. Help them identify opportunities to flourish.

KEY CONCEPT 3

OPPORTUNITY CAN BE FOUND IN CURRENT ROLES AND BEYOND.

No one knows what the future holds, but as a leader, you probably have a view of the organization your Top Talent does not. You can see future job openings, both within your team and across the organization. You can see cross-functional team assignments and project teams, which could be doorways to future roles.

THINGS YOU CAN DO TO PROMOTE OPPORTUNITY

☐ **SCOUTING SESSION**

Gather employee mentors from across the organization to host information sessions for your existing employees. The purpose: to showcase other opportunities and match employees with complementary interests or goals.

DATE COMPLETED: _____

☐ **EXPANDED VISION**

Create opportunities for employees to shadow other employees of similar tenure in a different department for a day.

DATE COMPLETED: _____

☐ DREAM SESSIONS

Schedule time with everyone on your team to discover their dreams. Then, as opportunities arise, help your people make their dreams become reality.

DATE COMPLETED: _____

☐ TRAVEL BUDDY

Look for an opportunity to take employees with you to meetings they might not normally attend, conferences they don't usually have access to, and other situations with an eye toward helping the employee see a Brighter Future.

DATE COMPLETED: _____

☐ OPEN SPACE

Design a physical workspace that encourages a fluid approach to learning and working. Explore open work environments that promote cross-functional development and facilitate dynamic, real-time growth.

DATE COMPLETED: _____

BIGGER VISION

SECTION THREE

Find a top performer and you will find a person who wants to be a part of something great. If you expect to attract the brightest and best, you are going to need a **BIGGER VISION.**

Top Talent wants to make a difference in the world. When Top Talent is considering where they will work, they typically have options. But make no mistake, they are more likely to work for an organization pursuing a **BIGGER VISION.**

For a full overview of Bigger Vision, please reference the Talent Magnet Field Guide.

BEST PRACTICE
ENSURE ALIGNMENT

When people in an organization work together, they set themselves apart. Clearly, alignment accelerates impact. Leaders who want to position their organizations to accomplish a Bigger Vision must **ENSURE ALIGNMENT;** only then can they harness the collective energy of those they lead. Without alignment, energy, productivity, and impact will suffer.

Choose to **ENSURE ALIGNMENT,** and you will be a step closer to becoming a place so attractive Top Talent will be standing in line to work for your organization.

KEY CONCEPT 1

PEOPLE ALWAYS WATCH THE LEADERS.

Leaders know they must model the way and continually work to train team members to embrace the vision, mission, values, systems, and strategy, if they hope to execute at a high level.

KEY CONCEPT 2

LEADERS ALIGN PEOPLE TO THE VISION.

Picture a tug of war. If leaders can get everyone in the organization on the same side of the rope, pulling together toward the goal, their competition is in trouble. If leaders succeed at aligning everyone to the culture, they also position themselves to be an employer of choice for Top Talent.

KEY CONCEPT 3

ALIGNMENT STRENGTHENS CULTURE.

Alignment permeates every aspect of a High Performance Organization. When everyone is in sync, the culture is fortified. This strength not only energizes existing team members, it multiplies your pull on Top Talent.

THINGS YOU CAN DO TO ENSURE ALIGNMENT

☐ NORTH STAR

Clarity is the prerequisite to alignment. Work with your leaders to ensure you agree on what matters most. This can be expressed in many ways - the most common: Vision or Mission, Core Values, and Goals.

DATE COMPLETED: _____

☐ 3 X 5 CARD

Test your alignment as a leadership team by passing out blank 3 x 5 cards. Ask a simple question: What matters most around here? (Or, any similar question of your liking) Compare your answers. It they don't match, you still have work to do.

DATE COMPLETED: _____

☐ CASCADING CHALLENGE

Leadership alignment is critical but insufficient. For the vision to have full power, it must be understood, embraced, and activated throughout your organization. Create a plan to ensure everyone knows the vision.

DATE COMPLETED: _____

☐ STRENGTHEN THE CHAIN

You are only as strong as your weakest link. Ask your employees to help you by identifying gaps and opportunities that impede the vision and values. Ask each person to help you strengthen the next link in the chain.

DATE COMPLETED: _____

☐ CONNECT TO WHY

Be diligent connecting the dots between what needs to be done functionally within the work and why it is important and meaningful to the organization and customers.

DATE COMPLETED: _____

BEST PRACTICE
FOSTER CONNECTION

Are your people connected to your vision? If not, this is bad news for your organization. A vision cannot be owned if it is not known. But, let's face it, there is something more important than knowing.

For a vision to move people to action, they must feel personally connected to it. That's why a leader has the responsibility to **FOSTER CONNECTION.**

KEY CONCEPT 1

GREAT PEOPLE ARE ATTRACTED TO GREAT CAUSES.

Research shows that top performers want to make a difference in the world … the kind of difference that cannot be accomplished alone. It's why they are attracted to organizations and teams who are passionate about a big vision.

KEY CONCEPT 2

WITHOUT PERSONAL CONNECTION, THE VISION IS IRRELEVANT.

If leaders can keep everyone personally connected to a grander cause beyond the business it is even better. The reach of a big vision might be global, but it doesn't have to be. The significance can be regional or even local. The point is, great people want to create great impact beyond profits and products.

KEY CONCEPT 3

LEADERS ARE RESPONSIBLE FOR MODELING THE VISION.

As the leader one of your primary responsibilities is to continually clarify, protect, and model the vision. If you do your best people will become ambassadors of influence. Additionally, your company will become a place where others want to be a part of the movement.

THINGS YOU CAN DO TO **FOSTER CONNECTION**

☐ SERVING DAY

Set aside a day with your team to engage in a mutually meaningful activity. Consider serving as volunteers for a local non-profit organization. You can even ask your team for recommendations.

DATE COMPLETED: _____

☐ NO COMPETITION DAY

Demonstrate the higher importance of community and social causes by joining forces with direct competitors to raise money or volunteer. This unexpected collaboration helps put business in a broader perspective.

DATE COMPLETED: _____

☐ ADOPT ANYTHING

Symbolic "adoptions" of kids in need, animals, parks, and other community causes can add a layer of shared meaning between employees that elevate the bonds made at work.

DATE COMPLETED: _____

☐ VISION CONNECT

At an upcoming meeting, ask a team member to share how and why he or she feels connected to the vision/mission of the organization. Repeat this activity often – vision leaks and so does meaningful connection.

DATE COMPLETED: _____

☐ SIGN ME UP!

Create a large poster or banner containing your vision/mission. Ask employees to literally "sign up" for the journey by writing their name on the sign. Display the signed banner where everyone on the team can see it often.

DATE COMPLETED: _____

BEST PRACTICE
CELEBRATE IMPACT

Celebration is one of the ways healthy organizations energize people, strengthen culture, and fuel performance. When we fail to CELEBRATE IMPACT as it relates to our vision, we undervalue the vision itself.

Your vision cannot only become a tremendous source of pride and motivation for your people, it can help draw potential like-minded employees to your organization. If you want to attract Top Talent, make it the norm to CELEBRATE IMPACT.

KEY CONCEPT 1

CELEBRATION AFFIRMS ACHIEVEMENT.

When leaders make time to celebrate, value is communicated and effort validated. These moments of celebration can also move the vision from the abstract to the tangible and fuel discretionary effort.

KEY CONCEPT 2

ACKNOWLEDGING WINS INSPIRES FUTURE RESULTS.

Celebration is a powerful performance-enhancing strategy. If leaders understand their unique role to empower, encourage, and praise people who help the organization move toward the vision and act on this knowledge, more wins are sure to follow.

KEY CONCEPT 3

FREQUENT CELEBRATION SHOULD BE THE NORM.

Repetition is the mother of learning. If you can create a culture where celebrating the vision is the norm, you can build a culture fueled by a passion to make the vision a reality. Tell stories often of the people who bring your vision to life.

THINGS YOU CAN DO TO CELEBRATE IMPACT

☐ STORY OF THE DAY

Establish stories as the currency of your team. End each shift or day by asking someone to share a personal accomplishment or impact moment from the day.

DATE COMPLETED: _____

☐ MORE THAN PROFITS

In addition to your traditional success metrics, sales, profits, etc., establish a measure or two you can track back to your Bigger Vision. Share your progress with the entire team.

DATE COMPLETED: _____

☐ VALUE OF THE WEEK

To create impact on a daily basis, focus on one of your core values each week. Then, be on the lookout for employee behaviors in alignment with that particular value. Recognize them! What gets recognized gets repeated.

DATE COMPLETED: _____

☐ CAUGHT DOING GOOD

Set up a box near your office where team members can submit (anonymously, if they prefer) short cards describing exemplary actions of other team members that uphold the organization's mission and values. Find ways to celebrate these people.

DATE COMPLETED: _____

☐ TEACH FOR IMPACT

Allow current employees to communicate, train, and onboard new employees. This allows everyone to appreciate and connect more fully with the vision and its impact.

DATE COMPLETED: _____

TELL THE STORY

SECTION FOUR

No matter how good you are, without creating awareness of what is going on in your organization, you receive no credit for your efforts.

Make the promise Top Talent wants to hear, keep it, and then make sure the people you are looking for know what they will get if they join your team. A magnet with a small surface area is weak as is your ability to attract Top Talent, unless you find new and creative ways to continually **TELL THE STORY.**

For a full overview of Tell the Story, please reference the Talent Magnet Field Guide.

BEST PRACTICE
BE PROACTIVE

Leaders who hope to build a Talent Magnet must **BE PROACTIVE** when it comes to sharing their employment promise. One of the first applications of this idea is to go outside the walls of your organization to spread the message.

A common misconception is that telling your employment story in orientation is sufficient; at that point, it's actually too late! Identify the places you want to recruit and go Tell the Story there; don't wait… initiate.

KEY CONCEPT 1

LEADERS WORK TO CREATE A STORY WORTH TELLING.

People love a good story – especially one in which they are the hero! Create an employee value proposition that makes Top Talent the hero and then work every day to make it true.

KEY CONCEPT 2

GREAT LEADERS ARE ALWAYS LOOKING FOR TOP TALENT.

Being proactive also means you are always on the lookout for great people. It is a recruiting mindset versus a hiring mindset; Leaders of Talent Magnets are always on the lookout and ready to offer a position to anyone considered Top Talent.

KEY CONCEPT 3

A RECRUITING BIAS IS ALWAYS PREFERRED TO A HIRING BIAS.

Those who hire often complain they never have enough people. Those who recruit are not looking for people, they are looking for great people and they know they will never have enough.

THINGS YOU CAN DO TO BE PROACTIVE

☐ OBSERVE AND CONNECT

When you experience Top Talent as a customer, speak up. Share what you observed about their work or service, and specify how valued they would be at your organization.

DATE COMPLETED: _____

☐ RECOGNIZE RESULTS

Carry cards that express your interest in having a conversation about a potential recruit's future. Reinforcing that you appreciate their talent, whether it is with your organization or otherwise, establishes you as someone whose intentions are about more than just hiring.

DATE COMPLETED: _____

☐ BE DIRECT

Ask, "What would it take to get someone of your caliber to work with us?" There is nothing more irresistible than knowing your work has been noticed and might be highly valued elsewhere.

DATE COMPLETED: _____

☐ CUSTOMER CHALLENGE

Invite promising recruits to sample your business as a customer. Express curiosity in receiving their opinion about your organization. The invitation immediately puts them in the mind frame of considering your organization as valuable and worthy of attention.

DATE COMPLETED: _____

☐ TALENT DEPTH CHART

If you anticipate any open positions in the coming months (or longer), create a plan that projects what your needs will be. Update your organizational depth chart and add positions you think might come open in the future.

DATE COMPLETED: _____

BEST PRACTICE
EMBRACE TECHNOLOGY

There are many ways to share the story of your Talent Magnet; however, one of the most powerful and far-reaching strategies to create awareness in today's world is to **EMBRACE TECHNOLOGY.** Thanks to the internet and social media, the world has become much smaller.

Many organizations struggle to find great people and yet never consider the picture they are painting through their use of technology. If you want to be relevant in today's marketplace and tell your story with greater reach and more impact, **EMBRACE TECHNOLOGY.**

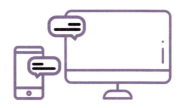

KEY CONCEPT 1

TECHNOLOGY CAN EXPONENTIALLY INCREASE YOUR REACH.

Not too many years ago, people would write letters by hand and mail them. Today, a single message or video can be shared with tens of millions instantaneously. Smart leaders are using this new global reach to recruit Top Talent.

KEY CONCEPT 2

SOCIAL MEDIA IS POWERFUL WHEN USED STRATEGICALLY.

Social media is the most powerful leadership tool in the history of the world. However, its powers are not guaranteed – only those who use it as a strategic communications channel reap its rewards. What is your objective? What key messages are you sending?

KEY CONCEPT 3

A MULTI-PLATFORM STRATEGY IS BEST.

What is your social media platform of choice? Ask ten people, and you are likely to receive ten different answers. There is no longer a single preferred channel of communications when searching for Top Talent.

THINGS YOU CAN DO TO **EMBRACE TECHNOLOGY**

☐ TECHNOLOGY AUDIT

Look at all the technology channels you currently employ to tell your story (Facebook, Twitter, Instagram, your website, etc.) Would Top Talent look at your messaging and decide you were a great place to work?

DATE COMPLETED:

☐ EDITORIAL CALENDAR

Map out your key messages around Better Boss, Brighter Future, and Bigger Vision and create a communications plan across all channels. Don't be random with your messaging and don't ignore key channels.

DATE COMPLETED:

☐ NOT MY JOB

Who on your team is accountable for using technology as a strategic communications tool? Consider allocating a portion of someone's job to fine-tune and disseminate your talent story.

DATE COMPLETED: _____

☐ LINK IT

A surprisingly overlooked and effective tactic for spreading your message online is to include links to your websites, Linkedin, and other social media pages in your email signature, business cards, and electronic contact cards.

DATE COMPLETED: _____

☐ INFUSE PERSONALITY

Much online content can be transactional or informative. People like to follow personalities and strong points of view, so feature individual voices that your audience can relate to.

DATE COMPLETED: _____

BEST PRACTICE
DEPUTIZE EVERYONE

Your chances of creating a Talent Magnet go up drastically if you can marshal the energy and effort of your entire organization; you cannot expect your leaders to carry the load alone.

DEPUTIZE EVERYONE to share this simple message… If you join our organization, you will find a Better Boss, a Brighter Future and a Bigger Vision.

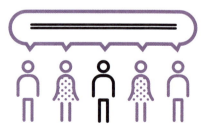

KEY CONCEPT 1

EXISTING EMPLOYEES CAN BE YOUR AMBASSADORS.

Your existing employees are your greatest ambassadors of your story. They are the ones who are helping create the culture and who are experiencing first hand the benefits of being on your team.

KEY CONCEPT 2

A CLEAR, TALENT-FOCUSED MESSAGE IS ESSENTIAL.

There is a reason the phrase "simple sells" has been repeated countless times over the generations – it is true. The story Top Talent wants to hear is simple. Our talent promise is: Better Boss, Brighter Future, and Bigger Vision.

KEY CONCEPT 3

TRAINING BUILDS COMPETENCE AND CONFIDENCE.

There is little more daunting than being charged to do something you are ill-equipped to do. No matter how passionate you may be about the work or the vision, without skills you will not be effective. Training turns intention into accomplishment.

THINGS YOU CAN DO TO DEPUTIZE EVERYONE

☐ KEEP SCORE

Establish a healthy competition among your existing team members regarding the number of referrals actually selected or the number of times a tweet or message about your talent story was shared or liked.

DATE COMPLETED: _____

☐ RECOGNIZE RESULTS

Offer training on how to tell your organization's talent story. Be sure you provide ample examples and illustrations to substantiate your promise: Better Boss, Brighter Future, and Bigger Vision.

DATE COMPLETED: _____

☐ CREATE RESOURCES

Don't expect the spoken word to always be sufficient. Create PowerPoint slides, video clips, and printed materials, to make it easier for your team members to Tell the Story well.

DATE COMPLETED: _____

☐ TRACK YOUR IMPACT

Add a little data science to your effort by using different approaches to Tell the Story and track your results. You may find for younger audiences, video creates a higher hit rate of inquiries, or for senior adults, printed material helps fuel interest.

DATE COMPLETED: _____

☐ INCENTIVIZE IMPACT

A simple framework can liberate the most hesitant employee when it comes to sharing a story. Try, "Context, Clarity, and Call to Action," as a simple three-part structure so employees can speak with confidence knowing what to say in their messaging.

DATE COMPLETED: _____

ADDITIONAL RESOURCES

TALENT MAGNET
HOW TO ATTRACT AND KEEP THE BEST PEOPLE

There is a long-standing truth in the world of organizations: talent wins! But how do you attract the best people? What do they really want? Based on rigorous and extensive research, the team learned that top performers are looking for very different things than solid contributors.

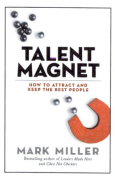

The team identified three critical aspects of a true Talent Magnet and explores the deeper meaning of each. He pulls back the curtain on what leaders can do to find and retain the very best people – a strategic need every leader faces.

TALENT MAGNET
FIELD GUIDE

The *Talent Magnet Field Guide* is a companion to the book, *Talent Magnet*. This resource gives an in-depth look at the three promises you need to make if you desire to become a place where Top Talent wants to work.

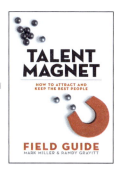

INTEGREAT APP

The InteGREAT Leadership app is a mobile experience designed to help leaders grow in four areas – lead self, lead others, lead teams, and lead organizations. Each bite-sized lesson is loaded with videos, assessments, and interactive experiences. If you are looking for an intentional process to grow your leadership, download the free InteGREAT Leadership app today!

**FOR MORE INFORMATION CONTACT:
INFO@INTEGREATLEADERSHIP.COM**